Tsukemono Recipes Cookbook

© Copyright 2020 by Y

MW00893814

Contents

ABOUT

Tsukemono, or Japanese pickles, are preserved vegetables that are pickled in salt, salt brine, or rice bran. They come in great varieties and forms, and you can often find one or two varieties of tsukemono being served in an Ichiju Sansai meal or as an accompaniment to sushi or as a garnish to a yoshoku (Japanese-western cuisine) dish like Japanese curry.

This Cookbook is a great source for various Tsukemono Recipes. Read on as I present to you, yummy and tasty Tsukemono's you can make at home.

YUMMY AND DELICIOUS HOME-MADE TSUKEMONO RECIPES

1. Sauerkraut Tsukemono

Yield: 4 Servings

Ingredients

- 50 g sauerkraut
- 1 knob fresh ginger, cut into thin stripes
- 50 g cucumber, cut into thin stripes
- 1 Tbsp canned tuna, drained
- to taste soy sauce
- 1 drizzle of sesame oil
- 1 pinch sesame seeds
- dry calendula petals you find for tea (optional)

Directions

1. Combine sauerkraut, ginger, cucumber and tuna in a bowl and season with soy sauce Adjust the amount of soy sauce depending on how much salt in your sauerkraut.
2. Drizzle the mixture with sesame oil. Sprinkle sesame seeds and calendula petals to garnish.

2. Instant Tsukemono (Pickles) - Chinese Cabbage Tossed in Garlic-Infused Kombu Tea

Ingredients

- 1/4 cut Chinese cabbage
- 1/2 tsp to 1 teaspoon Kombu tea
- 1 tsp Garlic (grated)
- 1 tsp Usukuchi soy sauce
- 1 Ichimi spice
- 1 tsp Salt (for pickling the cabbage)

Directions

1. Cut the Chinese cabbage into 1 cm widths. Salt and let sit for 5 minutes before squeezing out the water, making sure to remove all of it.
2. Put the Chinese cabbage in a bowl with the * ingredients and mix well.
3. It's done!

3. Vegetable Pickles or Tsukemono

Ingredients

- 1 Daikon or Mooli
- 1 chinese cabbage
- Vinegar mixture per 1 vegetable
- 1/2 cup sugar
- 3/4 cup white vinegar
- 1 lemon
- 1 cup warm water
- Pinch sea salt
- 1-2 big red chilli (optional)

Directions

1. Use one daikon. Peel the skin off.
2. Cut them into long chunks. Place them in a big container.
3. To make pickling marinade. Combine sugar, salt and vinegar until the sugar dissolves.
4. Add some lemon and mix all.
5. Pour the pickling marinade sauce in to the daikon. Cover with lid. Leave it over night at

room temperature. Ready to eat after 6 hours or the next day.

6. Do the same method with chinese canbage but cut your cabbage vertically.

4. Turnip Greens in Japanese Broth (kabu-ohitashi)
Yield: 4 Servings

Ingredients

- 1 bunch turnip greens in good condition
- 13-15 g finely shaved katsuo-bushi (bonito flakes for Japanese stock) (or 2 handfuls)
- 1 Tbsp cooking sake
- 1/2-1 tsp salt
- 2 tsp sesame oil
- 2 pinches fresh yuzu citrus zest/sliced yuzu skin

Directions

1. Trim turnip bulbs from greens. Wash the greens well and prepare a large pot of boiling water with a few pinches of salt.
2. When the water boils, put in the greens with the thicker stalk end first, then submerge the rest of the leaves part into the pot with chopsticks.
3. Cook for 30-60 seconds until the greens are bright green. Remove from boiling water and right away rinse in cold water so it stops cooking.

4. Drain, and gently squeeze out extra water and then cut the leaves into 5 cm pieces. Put aside for now.

5. Now let's make the Japanese dashi! You need about 13-15 grams (2 handfuls) of katsuobushi flakes. Or, if you have your own broth, just use 400 ml of that.

6. Bring 400 ml water to a boil. Add the katsuobushi flakes, turn the heat to low and simmer for 3 minutes. Stop the heat and let it set for 1 minute. Lastly strain out the flakes with a strainer/colander. Now you have dashi!

7. Put the dashi back into a medium pot. Add the salt, soy sauce and sake to the pot and bring to a boil. Turn to low. Add the turnip greens from before and when it boils again, stop the heat.

8. Put the greens into a large dish (or separate into everyone's bowls). Pour over some of the broth, a dash of sesame oil and if you have it, some thin slices of yuzu skin or zest.

5. Nappa Cabbage and Mustard Green Ohitashi
Yield: 2 Servings

Ingredients

- 150 g Nappa cabbage
- 50 g mustard greens
- 1 tsp miso
- 1 tsp mayonaise
- 1 tsp soy sauce
- 1 tsp sugar
- 1 tsp rice vinegar
- 1 tsp white sesame seeds

Directions

1. Slice the nappa cabbage into 1cm thick pieces. Cut mustard greens to about 4 cm in length.
2. Boil water in a pot with a pinch of salt. Put in all the vegetables and boil for less than one minute. Take out and drain for a while.
3. Mix the miso, mayonnaise, soy sauce, sugar, rice vinegar and sesame seeds to make the sauce.

4. When the vegetables have cooled, squeeze them to get rid of the excess water. Put into a bowl, add the sauce and mix well.

6. Instant Cabbage and Shio-Konbu Tsukemono Pickles
Yield: 2 Servings

Ingredients

- 2 leaves Cabbage
- 20 to 25 grams Shio-kombu
- 1/4 tsp Salt (a pinch)
- 1 tsp Ponzu
- 1 Shichimi spice

Directions

1. Rip up the cabbage leaves with your hands.
2. Sprinkle the cabbage with salt, and make the shio-konbu ready!
3. Put the cabbage and shio-konbu in a plastic or Ziploc bag.
4. Massage lightly over the bag (optional). Put the bag in the refrigerator, rest for 5 to 10 minutes and it's done!!
5. Transfer to a serving dish, sprinkle with ponzu sauce and shichimi spice, and enjoy!

7. Smoked Salmon, Gari and Avocado on Lightly Toasted Wholemeal Sourdough

Ingredients

- Slices smoked salmon
- Half an avocado per person
- Gari (Japanese pickled ginger)
- Wholemeal sourdough bread
- Soy sauce

Directions

1. Lightly toast the bread
2. Thinly slice the avocado and arrange on the toast
3. Top with the Salmon slices and then add a few slivers of the ginger (Gari)
4. Add a splash of soy sauce

8. Spinach OHITASHI

Ingredients

- 1 bag spinach
- 1 bag Katsuo Bushi
- 1 table spoon soup stock
- 1 table spoon soy source

Directions

1. Boil spinach quickly (1-2min).
2. Drain the water
3. Add soup stock, soy source and Katsuo Bushi
4. Mix everything together
5. Done

9. Puran Poli or Gari Rotli
Yield: 8 Servings

Ingredients

For Puran:

- 1 cup chana dal
- 3 cup water
- 1 cup sugar
- 1/4 tsp jaiphal powder / nutmeg powder
- 1/4 tsp cardamom powder / elachi powder

For Dough:

- 2 cup wheat flour / atta
- 1/2 cup maida / plain flour
- 1/4 tsp salt
- 2 tbsp oil
- as needed water to knead

Other Ingredients:

- 1/4 cup wheat flour / atta
- as needed oil/ghee for roasting

Directions

Puran preparation:

1. Firstly, in a large bowl take 1 cup chana dal and soak for 3 hours with enough water. few chana dal just need ½ hour of soaking.
2. Now in a pressure cooker, place a vessel pouring water at the bottom of cooker.
3. Transfer the soaked chana dal in cooker along with 3 cup water and 1 tsp oil.
4. Pressure cook on medium flame for 5 whistles.
5. Once the pressure settles down, open the cooker and drain off the water. allow resting for 30 minutes, making sure to drain off all the water from chana dal.
6. Take cooked chana dal in the kadai and add 1 cup of sugar.
7. Mix well until the sugar melts than add jaiphal powder and elaichi powder.
8. Continue to mix by mashing the chana dal.cook until the mixture thickens and starts to separate from the pan.

9. The mixture will start to hold the shape.Now puran is ready.

Dough preparation for puran poli.

1. Firstly, in a large mixing bowl take 2 cup wheat flour, ½ cup maida, 2tbsp oil and salt. mix well making sure everything is combined well.
2. Now add water as required and knead the dough well.
3. Knead to smooth and soft dough punching well.
4. Further grease 1 tsp of oil, cover and rest for 30 minutes.

Filling puran in poli to form puran poli:

1. firstly, pinch a ball sized dough and flatten well.also, pinch a ball sized puran (chana dal stuffing)
2. place the puran in center of dough.
3. stuff the puran and pinch off the excess dough securing tight.
4. furthermore, dust the ball with wheat flour and flatten with hand.

5. Roll in one direction making sure the puran poli is thin.

6. now put the rolled puran poli over hot tawa.

7. allow roasting on medium flame until it puffs up.

8. grease oil/ghee and flip over and cook both sides pressing slightly.

9. Finally, serve Gari Rotli with ghee

10. Wasabi 'Ohitashi' Marinated Spinach & Wakame
Yield: 4 Servings

Ingredients

- 1 bunch Spinach, 250 to 300g
- 5 g OR 2 tablespoons Dried Wakame
- 4 tablespoons 'Mentsuyu' OR Dashi Stock 2 tablespoons & Soy Sauce 2 tablespoons
- 1-2 teaspoons Wasabi Paste

Directions

1. Soak Dry Wakame in cold water until soft, drain well. Cut into smaller pieces if large.
2. Wash Spinach well and boil in boiling water until tender. Dip in cold water to stop cooking further, drain well and squeeze to remove excess water. Cut into 5cm length.
3. Place 'Mentsuyu' (OR Dashi Stock and Soy Sauce) and Wasabi in a bowl, mix well, then add prepared Spinach and Wakame, mix to combine.
4. Serve with extra Wasabi on top.

11. 'Ohitashi' Marinated Spinach & Nori
Yield: 4 Servings

Ingredients

- 1 bunch Spinach, 250 to 300g
- 2 sheets Toasted Nori, toasted just before adding to Spinach
- 4 tablespoons 'Mentsuyu' OR Dashi Stock
- 2 tablespoons & Soy Sauce 2 tablespoons
- Ginger 1 small piece, grated
- Dried Prawns 2 tablespoons, optional

Directions

1. Dried Prawns are optional. If you have, wash with water and soak in water for 1 to 2 hours to rehydrate. Cut to small pieces if large.
2. Wash Spinach well and boil in boiling water until tender. Dip in cold water to stop cooking further, drain well and squeeze to remove excess water. Cut into 5cm length.
3. Place prepared Spinach in a bowl, add rehydrated but still chewy Prawns, Ginger and

'Mentsuyu' (OR Dashi and Soy Sauce) and mix to combine.

4. Toast Nori sheets over flames even though they are toasted type, it will change the colour to green and very aromatic, then tear into small pieces and mix with the Spinach just before serving.

12. Pickled Fresh Ginger for Sushi (Gari)!
Yield: 1 Serving

Ingredients

- 150 grams Fresh ginger
- 1 pinch Salt
- 150 ml Vinegar
- 4 tbsp Sugar
- 1 tsp Salt

Directions

1. Wash the ginger, and peel it with a spoon. Use a mandoline/knife to slice against the grain to your preferred thickness.
2. Sprinkle with salt and rub it in, then let sit for 5-10 minutes to draw out the moisture. Rinse in water, and squeeze well. The volume will decrease.
3. Prepare the pickling liquid. Bring the ☆ ingredients to a boil, then stop the heat. Add to the ginger and mix. The ginger will turn slightly pink within 30 seconds.

13. Chikuwa Stuffed with Cheese, Cucumbers, and Takuan

Ingredients

- 6 Grilled chikuwa
- 1 Cucumber
- 1 Takuan (yellow pickled daikon)
- 1 Processed cheese

Directions

1. Cut the cucumbers, takuan, and cheese into the right thickness to fit the hole of chikuwa.
2. Cut into easy-to-eat pieces and serve.
3. So colorful. Serve with soy sauce or your favorite sauce.

14. Takuan (Yellow Pickled Daikon), Cucumber & Shiso Leaves Pasta

Yield: 3 Servings

Ingredients

- 300 grams Pasta
- 7 cm Takuan (5 mm cubes)
- 1 Cucumber (thinly sliced)
- 5 leaves Shiso leaves (julienned)
- 1 clove Garlic (thinly sliced)
- 3 tbsp Olive oil
- For the sauce:
- 3 tbsp Sake
- 2 1/2 tbsp each Soy sauce, mirin
- 100 ml Pasta water

Toppings:

- 1 Sesame oil, sesame seeds, lemon juice

Directions

1. Bring water to a boil to cook the pasta. Meanwhile, thinly slice the cucumber with a mandoline, and sprinkle with a little salt. When

the sliced cucumber has wilted, squeeze out the water. Cut the takuan and shiso leaves as well.

2. Add 2 tablespoons of salt (not listed) in the large pot of boiling water, and cook the pasta until al dente.

3. Put the olive oil and garlic in a frying pan, heat over low heat until fragrant, and add the sauce ingredients.

4. Add the cooked pasta, takuan, cucumber and shiso leaves to the frying pan from Step 3, and mix altogether over low heat.

5. Transfer the pasta and sauce to serving plates. Sprinkle with sesame oil and sesame seeds, and squeeze over some lemon juice to finish. Done.

15. Easy Dandelions with Sesame-flavored Takuan Pickles

Ingredients

- 1 sliced about 2 cm thick Takuan - Yellow pickled daikon
- 1 dash Sesame oil
- 1 several pieces Baby leaves
- 1 to your taste Toasted sesame seeds

Directions

1. Cut out a piece of takuan pickle about 3 cm in width. (Doesn't have to be a perfect circle.)
2. Insert cuts in a grid pattern without cutting all the way through. (Seefor reference)
3. Pat off moisture from Step 2 and shape into a flower. Brush on a thin layer of sesame oil.
4. Garnish with mesclun greens and serve. Sprinkle on some sesame seeds if you'd like.

16. Daikon Bettarazuke with Shio-koji

Ingredients

- 1/2 Daikon radish
- Pickling Liquid
- 1 4 tablespoons Shio-koji
- 1 [1 and 1/3 tablespoon] (Salt, if you don't have Shio-koji)
- 1 and 1/3 tablespoon Vinegar
- 1 tbsp Sake
- 90 grams Sugar

Directions

1. Cut the daikon radish into quarters lengthwise. (If the diameter is around 8 cm, just cut it into halves).
2. Peel the skin.
3. Combine the pickling liquid ingredients in a bowl, and microwave at 600 W for 40 seconds to dissolve the sugar. Mix well.
4. Using a large resealable plastic storage bag, combine the daikon from Step 2 and the pickling

liquid from Step 3. Make sure to remove as much air from the bag as possible to get the pickling liquid to coat the daikon.

5. Winter daikon is thick, so I cut it in quarters, but you can pickle an 8 cm diakon in halves.

6. Place it in a fridge and let it sit, flipping occasionally. It should be ready to eat after about 3 days.

7. Adjust the amount of shio-koji used.

17. Onigiri Rice Balls with Takuan and Mayonnaise
Yield: 1 Serving

Ingredients

- 1 Hot cooked rice
- 1 slice Takuan
- 1 tsp Mayonnaise
- 1 handful Bonito flakes
- 1 Nori seaweed

Directions

1. Chop the takuan roughly.
2. Combine rice, takuan, mayonnaise, and bonito flakes.
3. Mix thoroughly, and form into rice balls to finish.
4. Wrap up with nori if you'd like.

18. In Season Sweet Onion and Shio-koji Ohitashi

Ingredients

- 1 Sweet onion (medium)
- 1 dash less than 2 teaspoons ○ Shio-koji (salt fermented rice malt)
- 1 tsp ○ White sesame seeds
- 1 dash of each ○ Soy sauce + vinegar
- 1 generous amount, (to taste) Bonito flakes

Directions

1. Peel the onion, remove the top and bottom, and slice very thinly using a vegetable slicer.
2. Add the ○ ingredients with the onions, cover with plastic wrap and chill in the refrigerator for at least 10 minutes. The nutritious essence will seep out of the onions.
3. Transfer to serving plates, pour the liquid over, add a generous amount of bonito flakes and it's done.

19. Done In 5 Minutes! Delicious Spinach and Tuna Ohitashi
Yield: 4 Servings

Ingredients

- 1 bunch Spinach
- 80 grams Canned tuna
- 2 tbsp Soy sauce
- 2 tbsp Mirin
- 1 1/2 to 2 tablespoons Sesame oil

Directions

1. Wash the spinach, wrap it in plastic wrap and microwave. (I have a 'boiled vegetable' auto-setting on my microwave oven, but I think it should be about 1 and a half minutes at 500 W.)
2. Drain the oil from the canned tuna, and mix all the ingredients.
3. Squeeze out the moisture from the microwaved spinach and cut into 4 to 5 cm pieces. Combine with the seasoned tuna and it's done.

20. Kwadan gari(paropa)

Ingredients

- 200 g Gari
- Oil
- Ingredient(salt,Maggie,kuli-kuli)
- Onion,red pepper,small red pepper,green pepper

Directions

1. Suck and wash your gari live it to dry for just 2mint
2. Add a fresh vegetable to it and your ingredients turn well, pure the kuli-kuli into it and turn again
3. And also add a oil to it and turn it again uhmmm tasted so good and served.

21. Gari da gyada

Ingredients

- Garri
- G/nut
- Sugar n cold water

Direction

1. Remove d bark of ur g/nut until clean, mix all ingredients together with cold water, wow enjoy.

22. Gari with veggies

Ingredients

- Gari
- Maggie
- Mai
- Tomatoes
- Cabbage
- Water

Directions

1. In a bowl add all d ingredients
2. Then add your gari inside mix it and serve

Serves: 4-6

Prep Time: 15min

Cook Time: 10min

Ingredients

Pickled mushrooms

- 200 gmixed Asian mushrooms such as shiitake, shimeji and baby oyster
- 185 mlrice vinegar
- 1 tbspsoy sauce
- 1 tbspmirin
- 3 tspfinely shredded ginger
- 2-3 tspcaster sugar
- ½ tspinstant dashi powder (see note)
- ½ tspblack sesame seeds, toasted

Pickled spring onions

- 1 bunchspring onions, cut into 3 cm lengths

- ½ bunchred radish, sliced into thin wedges
- 185 ml(¾ cup) rice vinegar
- 60 ml(¼ cup) mirin
- 1-2 tspsalt
- 1 tspfinely grated ginger
- ½ tspsesame oil
- 10shiso leaves (see note), finely sliced

Miso cucumbers

- 300 gsmall cucumbers
- ½ cupred miso paste (see note)
- 1½ tbsprice vinegar
- 1 tbspmirin
- 1 tbspcooking sake (see note)
- 1clove garlic, crushed
- 1 tspsesame seeds, toasted

Directions

Pickling time 30 minutes

1. To make the pickled mushrooms, wipe the tops with a damp cloth to remove any dirt. Cut shiitake into thick slices and separate shimeji

and baby oyster mushrooms into single pieces. Combine rice vinegar, soy sauce, mirin, ginger, caster sugar, dashi powder and 80 ml (⅓ cup) water in a small saucepan. Bring to the boil, add mushrooms, reduce the heat and simmer for 4 minutes. Transfer the mixture to a clean bowl and place in the fridge for 30 minutes to cool. To serve, drain the liquid, transfer the mushrooms and ginger to a bowl and sprinkle over the sesame seeds.

2. To make the pickled spring onions, bring a medium-sized saucepan of well-salted water to the boil. Separate the thin green tips of the spring onion and set aside. Add the remaining spring onion to the saucepan and cook for 1 minute. Add the reserved tips, turn off the heat and steep for 30 seconds. Drain and refresh in cold water, then drain again. Combine the spring onions, radish, rice vinegar, mirin, salt, ginger, sesame oil, half the shiso leaves and 60 ml (¼ cup) water. Toss to combine, taste and adjust seasonings. Set aside for 30 minutes. To

serve, drain liquid, transfer spring onions and radish to a bowl, and top with remaining shiso.

3. To make the miso cucumbers, cut cucumbers lengthways into quarters then in half crossways. Combine the miso paste, rice vinegar, mirin, sake and garlic, and mix until smooth. Add the cucumbers and mix until well coated in the paste. Set aside for 30 minutes. To serve, remove the cucumbers from the miso cure and briefly rinse or wipe away almost all of the cure. Place the cucumbers in a bowl. Stir the miso cure to incorporate the cucumber water and drizzle lightly over the cucumbers. Sprinkle with sesame seeds.

24. Crunchy Tsukemono (Pickled Brinjal)

Ingredients

- 12 baby brinjals
- 4 halved beetroot, peeled and chopped
- 1 cup soya sauce
- 1 cup rice wine vinegar

Directions

1. Place all the ingredients into a medium saucepan.
2. Bring to the boil, cover and simmer until the vegetables are soft, about 20 minutes.
3. Cool in the liquid. Store in a Tupperware or Ziploc bag in the fridge.
4. They're delicious with the chicken katsu.

25. Fermented Napa Cabbage (Hakusai No Tsukemono)
Makes: 5 pounds (2 1/2 kilograms)

Ingredients

- 8 small heads Chinese cabbage, quartered vertically (about 1 1/3 pounds/600 grams each)
- 135 grams sea salt (3% cabbage weight)
- 8 small garlic cloves, thinly sliced
- 8 small dried Japanese (or 6 árbol) chile peppers
- Peeled strips from 4 small yuzu or Meyer lemons (avoid the white bitter pith)

Directions

1. Remove any outside wilted leaves of the cabbage. On sheets of newspaper set directly on the ground, dry the cabbage quarters for 1 day.
2. Line a plastic or wooden pickling tub with a large pickling-grade plastic bag. Pack one layer of the slightly dried Chinese cabbage, cut side down, on the bottom of the pickling container, rubbing each one with salt before you set it in the tub. Sprinkle the layer of cabbage with some of the

sliced garlic, chile peppers, and yuzu zest. Continue until all the cabbage quarters have been rubbed with salt and packed in the pickling tub. Don't forget to throw in some garlic, chile peppers, and yuzu peel before you start each new layer. Make sure the cabbage is snugly packed and flatten the excess portion of the plastic bag across the surface of the cabbage, pressing out the air to create a seal. Set the pickle tub's drop lid on top (or find a suitable substitute), weight with a rock or other heavy object (about the equivalent weight of the cabbage), and cover. Let sit outside in a cold shady spot, out of direct sunlight, for a couple of weeks. (Check after a few days to make sure enough brine has been exuded to cover the cabbage. If not, sprinkle in a little more salt.) If mold forms, lift it off the pickles gently and wipe any mold spots on the plastic bag or wooden tub with a neutral alcohol such as shochu or vodka.

3. The pickles can be eaten any time, but perhaps better to wait at least 2 weeks. They reach optimum flavor after 1 or 2 months, and stay

good while the cold weather holds (store in the refrigerator if the days turn warm).

26. Kyuri Tsukemono

Servings: 4

Ingredients

- 2 cucumbers
- 2 Tbsps soy sauce
- 1 Tbsp rice vinegar
- 1 tsp sesame oil
- Some red dried chili peppers

Directions

1. Rough chop cucumbers. In a medium, securely sealable container, combine soy sauce, rice vinegar, and sesame oil.
2. Add cucumbers to the marinade, close container and shake. Refrigerate for 1 to 2 hours. Shake cucumbers periodically, or leave overnight to marinate.

Note, the longer the cucumbers are left in the marinade the saltier they become. I've left them in the marinade for up to 3 days and the cucumbers were good. Serve and enjoy!

27. Sunomono

Prep Time: 15 Minutes

Cook Time: 10 Minutes

Total Time: 25 Minutes

Ingredients

- 3 Japanese cucumber or 2 English cucumber
- 1/2 teaspoon salt
- 1 cup dashi chilled
- 1/2 cup rice wine vinegar
- 1/4 cup sugar
- 1-2 tablespoon light soy sauce usukuchi shoyu
- 1/2 teaspoon salt
- 1 tablespoon natural sesame seeds toasted
- 1 teaspoon shichimi pepper Japanese spices

Directions

1. In a small saucepan, heat rice wine vinegar, sugar and ½ teaspoon of salt. When sugar is dissolved, turn the heat off and set it aside to cool.

2. Cut cucumbers lengthwise and remove seeds. Slice them crosswise very thin then put them in a medium bowl. Springle cucumber with ½ teaspoon of salt and set it aside for about 5-10 minutes.
3. When vinegar mixture is cold, mix it with dash and light soy sauce.
4. Squeeze salted cucumber to remove any excess water then add it to the vinegar mixture. Sprinkle cucumber with sesame and shichimi and put it in refrigerator to chill and pickle at least 30 minutes to an hour before serving.

28. Marinated Scallions -- Negi No Doresshingu Zuke
Servings: 8

Ingredients

- 4 tablespoons unseasoned rice vinegar
- 4 teaspoons whole grain mustard
- 1/2 teaspoon fine grain sea salt
- 1/4 teaspoon freshly ground black pepper
- 1 1/2 pounds scallions, white and light green parts cut into 2-inch long pieces

Directions

1. Whisk the arrowroot starch with a small amount of the water in a small saucepan. Once that is mixed, slowly whisk in the rest of the water. Bring the water to a boil over medium-high heat, then reduce the heat to maintain a simmer and continue simmering for 5 minutes. After 5 minutes, remove the saucepan from the heat and pour the liquid into a heat resistant container, like a glass jar and let it cool until it's

warm.   Cover the container with a lid and refrigerate. Once it is chilled, it is ready to use.

2. Once the arrowroot mixture has chilled, whisk in the rice vinegar, whole grain mustard, salt and pepper, then set aside.

3. In a saucepan fitted with a steamer basket, bring 1 inch of water to a boil. Add the scallions to the steamer basket, cover and steam until just tender. Steaming time will vary depending on how thick your scallions are, but begin checking them after 3 minutes of steaming time.

4. Drain the scallions and put them into a container for marinating. Pour the marinade immediately over the scallions and gently stir so that the scallions are completely coated.   Let the scallions cool before putting a lid on the container and putting it in the refrigerator to chill. The scallions are ready to eat once chilled. They will keep in the refrigerator for about a week.

29. Japanese-Style Turnip and Persimmon Pickle

Yield: 2 Servings

Prep Time: 15 Min

Total Time: 15 Min (Plus Several Hours for The Favors to Meld Together)

Ingredients

- ⅓ cup rice vinegar, plus more to taste
- 2 tsp sugar
- 7-8 baby turnips (200 g)
- 1 firm fuyu persimmon
- ½ tsp salt

Directions

1. To make the amazu, place the rice vinegar in a small bowl and stir in the sugar until dissolved. Set aside.
2. Trim the turnips and cut lengthwise through the root in half. Then slice crosswise into thin semicircular disks. Place in a bowl and toss with the salt. Set aside for 10 minutes until softened.

3. Peel the persimmon and slice into thin slivers.

4. Drain the turnips and place in a container along with the persimmon. Pour the amazu over and mix well. Cover and refrigerate for several hours before eating.

12270734R00033